CLASSIC
NURSERY RHYMES

CLASSIC
NURSERY RHYMES

Illustrated by
FREDERICK RICHARDSON

Beehive Books

A BEEHIVE BOOK

© Copyright 1972 Hubbard Press, Northbrook, Illinois, U.S.A.
Original title: The Classic Volland Edition – Mother Goose

First published in UK and Commonwealth 1984 by Purnell Books

Reprinted 1988 under the Black Cat imprint

This edition published 1993 in association with
Simon & Schuster Young Books
Campus 400
Maylands Avenue
Hemel Hempstead
Herts HP2 7EZ

ISBN 0 7500 9027 8
Printed in the Slovak Republic
52 197/2

INTRODUCING

Purnell's Book of

NURSERY RHYMES

Ever since I was a little girl of four and owned my first Book of Nursery Rhymes, I have had a warm and constant affection for these wonderful rhymes.

In this remarkable edition, every child will discover the enduring quality of nursery rhymes, with their happy mixture of anecdote and pure fantasy.

Long before small boys and girls are ready for the "Once upon a time" stories, they will listen, with absorbed attention, to nursery rhymes. Without effort, a child, as he listens to the rhymes and looks at the pictures, readily and painlessly discovers the magic of words. He can reach out, far beyond the confines of the nursery, to cats and queens, to old women sweeping cobwebs from the sky, and to black hens

which lay eggs for gentlemen.

Favourites apart, there are the ABC rhymes and the counting rhymes which may be repeated again and again without fear of boredom.

My advice to young mothers would be to learn some of these rhymes by heart if they do not already know them. They would then have a store of sparkling funny thoughts to raid in times of stress.

Unlike the old woman in the shoe who had so many children she didn't know what to do, mothers need never be at a loss if they are master-hands at quoting nursery rhymes!

And to those who would lay aside such an entertaining, soothing book for something more learned, this book sweetly and mildly answers, "Fudge".

JANE CARRUTH

FOREWORD

by SIR JOHN BETJEMAN

Nursery rhymes are the first poetry we know. Rhyme and rhythm are easy to learn and quicker and shorter than prose. Sense matters less than the music the words make when they are spoken out loud. Nursery rhymes sing in the head before ever we learn to read. And if we don't quite know what they mean, it doesn't matter; the rhythm and the jingle stay for life. Poetry comes first, prose comes later. How can you have free verse if you don't first know what you're freeing yourself from?

There are lots of rhymes in this book I have never read before and there are others with lines which differ a little from the version I learned as a child. But this is what a nursery rhyme book ought to be. Every page is a surprise and you don't know what you're going to see when you turn over to the next. The feel and look of the book is good, for it was originally published in the spacious days before 1914, when margins were broad and colours were bright and trouble was taken over details. The book is stoutly bound and sewn, and well made to resist jammy fingers and constant turning over to find a favourite page.

Frederick Richardson, who drew the illustrations, died in about 1926. Some of these illustrations have the slightly

alarming quality which suggests there is another world besides the one in which we live. They also play about with scale and give human qualities to things like cooking pots and wooden spoons.

Even if you don't know what the rhyme means you can always hear its rhythm and where there is an illustration the meaning is made quite clear, as when the cow jumped over the moon and Jack Horner pulled out a plum with his thumb from a Christmas pie.

I like to think that this book will inspire children and make them take to poetry, which is natural, before they are contaminated by prose, which is not. This edition takes poets under its wing and teaches us our alphabets and the power words have to make themselves loved and remembered.

Any edition like this makes books a pleasure and something to keep and hand down to the next generation.

Old Mother Goose, when
She wanted to wander,
Would ride through the air
On a very fine gander.

OLD MOTHER GOOSE

Old Mother Goose, when
　　She wanted to wander,
Would ride through the air
　　On a very fine gander.

Mother Goose had a house,
　　'Twas built in a wood,
An owl at the door
　　For a porter stood.

She had a son Jack,
　　A plain-looking lad,
He was not very good,
　　Nor yet very bad.

She sent him to market,
　　A live goose he bought:
"Here! mother," says he,
　　"It will not go for nought."

Jack's goose and her gander
　　Grew very fond;
They'd both eat together,
　　Or swim in one pond.

Jack found one morning,
　　As I have been told,
His goose had laid him
　　An egg of pure gold.

Jack rode to his mother,
　　The news for to tell.
She called him a good boy,
　　And said it was well.

And Old Mother Goose
　　The goose saddled soon,
And mounting its back,
　　Flew up to the moon.

There was a crooked man,
And he went a crooked mile,
He found a crooked sixpence
Against a crooked stile;
He bought a crooked cat
Which caught a crooked mouse,
And they all lived together
In a little crooked house.

The north wind doth blow,
And we shall have snow,
And what will poor robin do then?
                              Poor thing!

He'll sit in the barn
And keep himself warm,
And hide his head under his wing.
                              Poor thing!

Cock-a-doodle-doo,
My dame has lost her shoe:
My master's lost his fiddlestick,
And knows not what to do.

Peter, Peter, pumpkin eater,
Had a wife and couldn't keep her;
He put her in a pumpkin shell,
And then he kept her very well.

Peter, Peter, pumpkin eater,
Had another, and didn't love her;
Peter learned to read and spell,
And then he loved her very well.

I had a little hobby-horse,
And it was dapple grey;
Its head was made of pea-straw,
Its tail was made of hay.
I sold it to an old woman
For a copper groat;
And I'll not sing my song again
Without another coat.

❦

Monday's bairn is fair of face,
Tuesday's bairn is full of grace,
Wednesday's bairn is full of woe,
Thursday's bairn has far to go,
Friday's bairn is loving and giving,
Saturday's bairn works hard for its
    living;
But the bairn that is born on the
    Sabbath day
Is bonny and blithe and good and
    gay.

❦

Three young rats with black felt
    hats,
Three young ducks with white
    straw flats,
Three young dogs with curling
    tails,
Three young cats with demi-veils,
Went out to walk with three
    young pigs
In satin vests and sorrel wigs;
But suddenly it chanced to rain
And so they all went home again.

"Billy, Billy, come and play,
While the sun shines bright as day."

"Yes, my Polly, so I will,
For I love to please you still."

"Billy, Billy, have you seen
Sam and Betsy on the green?"

"Yes, my Poll, I saw them pass,
Skipping o'er the new-mown grass."

"Billy, Billy, come along,
And I will sing a pretty song."

❦

Hie to the market, Jenny come trot,
Spilt all her buttermilk, every drop,
Every drop and every dram,
Jenny came home with an
    empty can.

❦

Shoe the colt,
Shoe the colt,
Shoe the wild mare;
Here a nail,
There a nail,
Colt must go bare.

❦

If all the world were apple pie,
    And all the sea were ink,
And all the trees were bread and
    cheese,
    What should we have to drink?

Lady-bird, Lady-bird,
Fly away home,
Your house is on fire,
Your children will burn.

One misty, moisty morning,
When cloudy was the weather,
I chanced to meet an old man clothed all in leather.
He began to compliment, and I began to grin,
How do you do, and how do you do?
And how do you do again?

I like little pussy, her coat is so warm,
And if I don't hurt her she'll do me no harm;
So I'll not pull her tail, nor drive her away,
But pussy and I very gently will play.

Little Bo-peep has lost her sheep,
And can't tell where to find them;
Leave them alone, and they'll come home,
And bring their tails behind them.

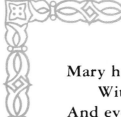

Mary had a little lamb
    With fleece as white as snow.
And everywhere that Mary went
    The lamb was sure to go.

It followed her to school one day —
    That was against the rule.
It made the children laugh and
      play
    To see a lamb at school.

And so the teacher turned it out,
    But still it lingered near,
And waited patiently about
    Till Mary did appear.

"Why does the lamb love Mary so?"
    The eager children cry.
"Why, Mary loves the lamb, you
      know!"
    The teacher did reply.

Birds of a feather flock together,
And so will pigs and swine;
Rats and mice have their choice,
And so will I have mine.

Go to bed first,
A golden purse;
Go to bed second,
A golden pheasant;
Go to bed third,
A golden bird.

My mother said, I never should
Play with the gypsies in the wood.
If I did, then she would say:
Naughty girl to disobey.
Your hair shan't curl and your
    shoes shan't shine,
You gypsy girl you shan't be mine.
And my father said that if I did,
He'd rap my head with the teapot
    lid.

My mother said that I never should
Play with the gypsies in the wood.
The wood was dark, the grass was
    green;
By came Sally with a tambourine.
I went to sea — no ship to get
    across;
I paid ten shillings for a blind
    white horse.
I upped on his back and was off
    in a crack,
Sally tell my mother I shall never
    come back.

There's a neat little clock, —
In the schoolroom it stands, —
And it points to the time
With its two little hands.

And may we, like the clock,
Keep a face clean and bright,
With hands ever ready
To do what is right.

Little Nanny Etticoat
In a white petticoat,
    And a red nose;
The longer she stands
    The shorter she grows.

Jack, be nimble; Jack, be quick;
Jack, jump over the candlestick.

Who killed Cock Robin?
"I," said the sparrow,
"With my little bow and arrow,
I killed Cock Robin."

Who saw him die?
"I," said the fly,
"With my little eye,
I saw him die."

Who caught his blood?
"I," said the fish,
"With my little dish,
I caught his blood."

Who'll make his shroud?
"I," said the beetle,
"With my thread and needle.
I'll make his shroud."

Who'll carry the torch?
"I," said the linnet,
"I'll come in a minute,
I'll carry the torch."

Who'll be the clerk?
"I," said the lark,
"If it's not in the dark,
I'll be the clerk."

Who'll dig his grave?
"I," said the owl,
"With my spade and trowel
I'll dig his grave."

Who'll be the parson?
"I," said the rook,
"With my little book,
I'll be the parson."

Who'll be chief mourner?
"I," said the dove,
"I mourn for my love,
I'll be chief mourner."

Who'll sing a psalm?
"I," said the thrush,
"As I sit in a bush.
I'll sing a psalm."

Who'll carry the coffin?
"I," said the kite,
"If it's not in the night,
I'll carry the coffin."

Who'll toll the bell?
"I," said the bull,
"Because I can pull,
I'll toll the bell."

All the birds of the air
Fell sighing and sobbing,
When they heard the bell toll
For poor Cock Robin.

Rain, rain, go away,
Come again another day;
Little Johnny wants to play.

Pretty John Watts,
We are troubled with rats.
Will you drive them out of the house?
We have mice, too, in plenty,
That feast in the pantry,
But let them stay
And nibble away,
What harm in a little brown mouse?

I'll tell you a story
About Mary Morey,
And now my story's begun.
I'll tell you another
About her brother,
And now my story's done.

Hush-a-bye, Baby, upon the tree top,
When the wind blows the cradle will rock;
When the bough breaks the cradle will fall,
Down tumbles cradle and Baby and all.

Ride away, ride away,
   Johnny shall ride,
And he shall have pussy-cat
   Tied to one side;
And he shall have little dog
   Tied to the other,
And Johnny shall ride
   To see his grandmother.

Little Jenny Wren fell sick,
Upon a time;
In came Robin Redbreast
And brought her cake and wine.

"Eat well of my cake, Jenny,
Drink well of my wine."
"Thank you, Robin, kindly,
You shall be mine."

Jenny she got well,
And stood upon her feet,
And told Robin plainly
She loved him not a bit.

Robin being angry,
Hopped upon a twig,
Saying, "Out upon you! Fie upon
    you!
Bold-faced jig!"

Dance, little baby, dance up high!
Never mind, baby, mother is by.
Crow and caper, caper and crow,
There, little Baby, there you go!

Up to the ceiling, down to the
    ground,
Backwards and forwards, round
    and round;
Dance, little baby and mother will
    sing,
With the merry coral, ding, ding,
    ding!

There was an old woman of
    Gloucester,
Whose parrot two guineas it cost
    her,
But its tongue never ceasing,
Was vastly displeasing
To the talkative woman of
    Gloucester.

I am a pretty wench,
    And I come a great way
        hence,
And sweethearts I can get
        none:
    But every dirty sow
    Can get sweethearts enough,
And I pretty wench can get
        none.

What are little boys made of,
    made of?
What are little boys made of?
Snaps and snails and puppy dogs
        tails;
And that's what little boys are
        made of, made of.

What are little girls made of,
    made of?
What are little girls made of?
Sugar and spice and all that's nice;
And that's what little girls are
        made of, made of.

Dickery, dickery, dock,
The mouse ran up the clock;
The clock struck one,
The mouse ran down,
Dickery, dickery, dock.

A, B, C, D, E, F, G,
H, I, J, K, L, M, N, O, P,
Q, R, S, and T, U, V,
W, X, and Y and Z.
Now I've said my A, B, C,
Tell me what you think of me.

The little robin grieves
    When the snow is on the ground,
For the trees have no leaves,
    And no berries can be found.

The air is cold, the worms are hid;
    For robin here what can be done?
Let's strow around some crumbs of bread,
    And then he'll live till snow is gone.

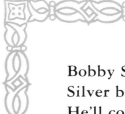

Bobby Shaftoe's gone to sea,
Silver buckles on his knee;
He'll come back and marry me,
      Pretty Bobby Shaftoe.

Bobby Shaftoe's fat and fair,
Combing down his yellow hair,
He's my love forevermore,
      Pretty Bobby Shaftoe.

See-saw, sacradown,
Which is the way to London town?
One foot up, the other foot down,
That is the way to London town.

A cat came fiddling out of a barn,
With a pair of bagpipes under her
    arm;
She could sing nothing but fiddle-
    de-dee,
The mouse has married the
    bumble-bee;
Pipe, cat — dance, mouse —
We'll have a wedding at our good
    house.

Little Betty Blue
Lost her holiday shoe.
What will poor Betty do?
Why, give her another
To match the other,
And then she will walk in two.

Robin Hood, Robin Hood,
Is in the mickle wood!
Little John, Little John,
He to the town is gone.

Robin Hood, Robin Hood,
Telling his beads,
All in the greenwood
Among the green weeds.

Little John, Little John,
If he comes no more,
Robin Hood, Robin Hood,
We shall fret full sore!

There was a lady loved a swine,
Honey, quoth she,
Pig-hog wilt thou be mine?
Hoogh, quoth he.

I'll build thee a silver sty,
Honey, quoth she,
And in it thou shalt lie.
Hoogh, quoth he.

Pinned with a silver pin,
Honey, quoth she,
That thou may go out and in.
Hoogh, quoth he.

Wilt thou have me now,
Honey? quoth she.
Speak or my heart will break.
Hoogh, quoth he.

Little Tommy Tittlemouse
Lived in a little house;
He caught fishes
In other men's ditches.

About the bush, Willie, about the bee-hive,
About the bush, Willie, I'll meet thee alive.

Bah, bah, black sheep,
      Have you any wool?
Yes, marry, have I,
      Three bags full;
One for my master,
      One for my dame,
But none for the little boy
      Who cries in the lane.

Hickety, pickety, my black hen,
She lays eggs for gentlemen:
Gentlemen come every day
To see what my black hen doth lay.

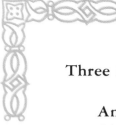

Three little kittens lost their
          mittens,
     And they began to cry,
     Oh! mother dear, we very
          much fear
     That we have lost our mittens.
Lost your mittens! You naughty
          kittens!
     Then you shall have no pie.
          Mee-ow, mee-ow, mee-ow.
     No, you shall have no pie.
          Mee-ow, mee-ow, mee-ow.

The three little kittens found their
          mittens,
     And they began to cry,
     Oh! mother dear, see here, see
          here,
     See, we have found our
          mittens.
Put on your mittens, you silly
          kittens,
     And you may have some pie.
          Purr-r, purr-r, purr-r,
     Oh! let us have the pie,
          Purr-r, purr-r, purr-r.

The three little kittens put on
          their mittens,
     And soon ate up the pie;
     Oh! mother dear, we greatly
          fear
     That we have soiled our
          mittens.

Soiled your mittens! you naughty
          kittens!
     Then they began to sigh,
          Mee-ow, mee-ow, mee-ow.
     Then they began to sigh,
          Mee-ow, mee-ow, mee-ow.

The three little kittens washed
          their mittens,
     And hung them out to dry;
     Oh! mother dear, do you not
          hear,
     That we have washed our
          mittens.
Washed your mittens! Oh! you're
          good kittens.
     But I smell a rat close by.
          Hush! hush! mee-ow.
          mee-ow.
     We smell a rat close by,
          Mee-ow, mee-ow, mee-ow.

Tweedle-dum and Tweedle-dee
Resolved to have a battle,
For Tweedle-dum said Tweedle-
          dee
Had spoiled his nice new rattle.
Just then flew by a monstrous
          crow,
As big as a tar barrel,
Which frightened both the
          heroes so,
They quite forgot their quarrel.

Willie boy, Willie boy,
    Where are you going?
O, let us go with you
    This sunshiny day.

I'm going to the meadow
    To see them a-mowing,
I'm going to help the girls
    Turn the new hay.

Three children sliding on the ice
    Upon a summer's day,
As it fell out, they all fell in,
    The rest they ran away.

Oh, had these children been at school,
    Or sliding on dry ground,
Ten thousand pounds to one penny
    They had not then been drowned.

Ye parents who have children dear,
    And ye, too, who have none,
If you would keep them safe abroad,
    Pray keep them safe at home.

Wee Willie Winkie runs through the town,
Upstairs and downstairs, in his nightgown;
Tapping at the window, crying at the lock:
"Are the babes in their beds, for it's now ten o'clock?

There was an old woman who lived in a shoe,
She had so many children she didn't know what to do.
She gave them some broth without any bread,
She whipped them all soundly and put them to bed.

Peter Piper picked a peck of
    pickled peppers;
A peck of pickled peppers Peter
    Piper picked.
If Peter Piper picked a peck of
    pickled peppers,
Where's the peck of pickled
    peppers
Peter Piper picked?

When I was a little girl,
About seven years old,
I hadn't got a petticoat,
To cover me from the cold.

So I went into Darlington,
That pretty little town,
And there I bought a petticoat,
A cloak, and a gown.

I went into the woods
And built me a kirk,
And all the birds of the air,
They helped me to work.

The hawk with his long claws
Pulled down the stone,
The dove with her rough bill
Brought me them home.

The parrot was the clergyman,
The peacock was the clerk,
The bullfinch played the organ,
We made merry work.

Here we go round the mulberry
    bush,
The mulberry bush, the mulberry
    bush,
Here we go round the mulberry
    bush.
On a cold and frosty morning.

This is the way we wash our
    hands,
Wash our hands, wash our hands,
This is the way we wash our
    hands,
On a cold and frosty morning.

This is the way we wash our
    clothes.
Wash our clothes, wash our
    clothes,
This is the way we wash our
    clothes,
On a cold and frosty morning.

This is the way we go to school,
Go to school, go to school,
This is the way we go to school,
On a cold and frosty morning.

This is the way we come out of
    school,
Come out of school, come out of
    school,
This is the way we come out of
    school,
On a cold and frosty morning.

There was a man and he had naught,
    And robbers came to rob him;
He crept up to the chimney top,
    And then they thought they had him.
But he got down on the other side,
    And then they could not find him;
He ran fourteen miles in fifteen days,
    And never looked behind him.

There was an old man,
And he had a calf,
And that's half;
He took him out of the stall,
And put him on the wall,
And that's all.

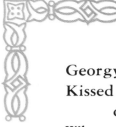

Georgy Porgy, pudding and pie,
Kissed the girls and made them
   cry.
When the boys came out to play,
Georgy Porgy ran away.

"Where are you going to, my pretty
   maid?"
"I'm going a-milking, sir," she said.
"May I go with you, my pretty
   maid?"
"You're kindly welcome, sir," she
   said.
"What is your father, my pretty
   maid?"
"My father's a farmer, sir," she
   said.
"What is your fortune, my pretty
   maid?"
"My face is my fortune, sir," she
   said.
"Then I can't marry you, my pretty
   maid!"
"Nobody asked you, sir!" she said.

My Maid Mary she minds the
   dairy,
While I go a-hoeing and mowing
   each morn;
Gaily run the reel and the little
   spinning wheel.
While I am singing and mowing
   my corn.

Dear, dear! what can the matter be?
Two old women got up in an
   apple tree;
One came down, and the other
   stayed till Saturday.

If all the seas were one sea,
What a great sea that would be!
And if all the trees were one tree,
What a great tree that would be!
And if all the axes were one axe,
What a great axe that would be!
And if all the men were one man,
What a great man he would be!
And if the great man took the
   great axe,
And cut down the great tree,
And let it fall into the great sea,
What a splish splash that would be!

Thirty white horses upon a red
   hill,
Now they tramp, now they champ,
Now they stand still.

A wise old owl sat in an oak,
The more he heard the less he
   spoke;
The less he spoke the more he
   heard.
Why aren't we all like that wise
   old bird?

Bow, wow, wow!
Whose dog art thou?
Little Tom Tinker's dog,
Bow, wow, wow!

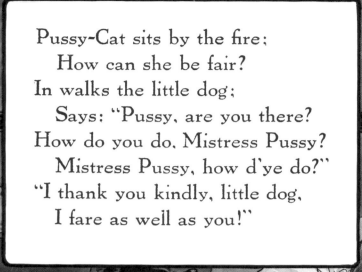

Pussy-Cat sits by the fire;
How can she be fair?
In walks the little dog;
Says: "Pussy, are you there?
How do you do, Mistress Pussy?
Mistress Pussy, how d'ye do?"
"I thank you kindly, little dog,
I fare as well as you!"

Here am I, little jumping Joan,
When nobody's with me
I'm always alone.

Jog on, jog on, the footpath way,
    And merrily jump the style,
        boys;
A merry heart goes all the day,
    Your sad one tires in a mile,
        boys.

⁂

There was an old woman had
        three sons,
Jerry and James and John,
Jerry was hanged, James was
        drowned,
John was lost and never was
        found;
And there was an end of her three
        sons,
Jerry and James and John!

⁂

Every lady in this land
Has twenty nails, upon each hand
Five, and twenty on hands and
        feet:
All this is true, without deceit.

⁂

Over the water, and over the sea,
And over the water to Charley,
I'll have none of your nasty beef,
Nor I'll have none of your barley;
But I'll have some of your very
        best flour
To make a white cake for my
        Charley.

Johnny shall have a new bonnet,
    And Johnny shall go to the
        fair,
And Johhny shall have a blue
        ribbon
    To tie up his bonny brown
        hair.
And why may not I love Johnny?
    And why may not Johnny love
        me?
And why may not I love Johnny,
    As well as another body?
And here's a leg for a stocking,
    And here's a leg for a shoe,
And here's a kiss for his daddy,
    And two for his mammy, I
        trow.
And why may not I love Johnny?
    And why may not Johnny love
        me?
And why may not I love Johnny,
    As well as another body?

⁂

There were once two cats of
        Kilkenny.
Each thought there was one cat
        too many;
So they fought and they fit,
And they scratched and they bit,
Till, excepting their nails,
And the tips of their tails,
Instead of two cats, there weren't
        any.

There was an old woman lived under the hill,
And if she's not gone she lives there still.
Baked apples she sold, and cranberry pies,
And she's the old woman that never told lies.

Simple Simon met a pieman
  Going to the fair;
Says Simple Simon to the pieman:
  "Pray let me taste your ware."

Says the pieman to Simple Simon:
  "Show me first your penny;"
Says Simple Simon to the pieman:
  "Indeed I have not any."

Sing a song of sixpence, a bag full of rye,
Four and twenty blackbirds baked in a pie;
When the pie was opened the birds began to sing,
And wasn't this a dainty dish to set before the king?
The king was in the parlour counting out his money;
The queen was in the kitchen eating bread and honey;
The maid was in the garden hanging out the clothes,
There came a little blackbird and nipped off her nose.

To market, to market, to buy a fat pig,
Home again, home again, jiggety, jig.

Ride a cock horse
To Banbury Cross
To see what Tommy can buy:
A penny white loaf,
A penny white cake,
And a two-penny apple pie.

Little Tee Wee,
He went to sea
In an open boat;
And while afloat
The little boat bended,
And my story's ended.

Intery, mintery, cutery-corn,
Apple seed and apple thorn;
Wire, brier, limber-lock,
Five geese in a flock,
Sit and sing by a spring,
O-u-t, and in again.

Who made the pie?
I did.
Who stole the pie?
He did.
Who found the pie?
She did.
Who ate the pie?
You did.
Who cried for pie?
We all did.

Elizabeth, Elspeth, Betsy and Bess,
They all went together to seek a
    bird's nest;
They found a bird's nest with five
    eggs in it,
They all took one and left four
    in it.

Little girl, little girl, where have
    you been?
Gathering roses to give to the
    queen.
Little girl, little girl, what gave
    she you?
She gave me a diamond as big as
    my shoe.

Jerry Hall, he was so small,
A rat could eat him, hat and all.

There was a man of double deed,
Sowed his garden full of seed.
When the seed began to grow,
'Twas like a garden full of snow;

When the snow began to melt,
'Twas like a ship without a belt;
When the ship began to sail,
'Twas like a bird without a tail;

When the bird began to fly,
'Twas like an eagle in the sky;
When the sky began to roar,
'Twas like a lion at the door;

When the door began to crack,
'Twas like a stick across my back;
When my back began to smart,
'Twas like a penknife in my heart;
When my heart began to bleed,
'Twas death and death and
    death indeed.

Little Miss Muffet
Sat on a tuffet,
Eating some curds and whey;
There came a great spider,
And sat down beside her,
And frightened Miss Muffet away.

Three wise men of Gotham
Went to sea in a bowl,
And if the bowl had been stronger
My song had been longer.

There were two birds sat upon a stone,
Fal de ral—al de ral—laddy.
One flew away and then there was one,
Fal de ral—al de ral—laddy.
The other flew after and then there was none,
Fal de ral—al de ral—laddy.
So the poor stone was left all alone,
Fal de ral—al de ral—laddy.
One of these little birds back again flew,
Fal de ral—al de ral—laddy.
The other came after and then there were two,
Fal de ral—al de ral—laddy.
Says one to the other: "Pray, how do you do?"
Fal de ral—al de ral—laddy.
"Very well, thank you, and pray how are you?"
Fal de ral—al de ral—laddy.

This is the house that Jack built.
This is the malt
That lay in the house that Jack
   built.
This is the rat,
That ate the malt
That lay in the house that Jack
   built.
This is the cat,
That killed the rat,
That ate the malt
That lay in the house that Jack
   built.
This is the dog,
That worried the cat,
That killed the rat,
That ate the malt
That lay in the house that Jack
   built.

This is the cow with the crumpled
   horn,
That tossed the dog,
That worried the cat,
That killed the rat,
That ate the malt
That lay in the house that Jack
   built.
This is the maiden all forlorn,
That milked the cow with the
   crumpled horn,
That tossed the dog,
That worried the cat,
That killed the rat,
That ate the malt
That lay in the house that Jack
   built.
This is the man all tattered and
   torn,
That kissed the maiden all forlorn,
That milked the cow with the
   crumpled horn,
That tossed the dog,
That worried the cat,
That killed the rat,
That ate the malt
That lay in the house that Jack
   built.

This is the priest all shaven and
    shorn,
That married the man all tattered
    and torn,
That kissed the maiden all forlorn,
That milked the cow with the
    crumpled horn,
That tossed the dog,
That worried the cat,
That killed the rat,
That ate the malt
That lay in the house that Jack
    built.
This is the cock that crowed in
    the morn,
That waked the priest all shaven
    and shorn,
That married the man all tattered
    and torn,
That kissed the maiden all forlorn,
That milked the cow with the
    crumpled horn,
That tossed the dog,
That worried the cat,
That killed the rat,
That ate the malt
That lay in the house that Jack
    built.

This is the farmer sowing the corn,
That kept the cock that crowed in
    the morn.
That waked the priest all shaven
    and shorn,
That married the man all tattered
    and torn,
That kissed the maiden all forlorn,
That milked the cow with the
    crumpled horn,
That tossed the dog,
That worried the cat,
That killed the rat,
That ate the malt
That lay in the house that Jack
    built.

Bye, Baby bunting,
Father's gone a-hunting,
Mother's gone a-milking,
Sister's gone a-silking,
And Brother's gone to buy a skin
To wrap the Baby bunting in.

Little Polly Flinders
Sat among the cinders
   Warming her pretty little toes;
Her mother came and caught her,
Whipped her little daughter
   For spoiling her nice new clothes.

Boys and girls come out to play,
The moon doth shine as bright as
    day,
Leave your supper and leave your
    sleep,
And meet your playfellows in the
    street;
Come with a whoop and come with
    a call,
And come with a good will, or not
    at all.
Up the ladder and down the wall,
A halfpenny roll will serve us all.
You find milk and I'll find flour,
And we'll have a pudding in half
    an hour.

There was a little man,
    And he had a little gun,
And his bullets were made of lead,
    lead, lead;
    He went to the brook,
    And saw a little duck,
And shot it through the head, head,
    head.

    He carried it home
    To his good wife Joan,
And bade her a fire to make, make,
    make;
    To roast the little duck
    He had shot in the brook,
And he'd go fetch the drake, drake,
    drake.

A was an Apple pie;
    B bit it;
        C cut it;
            D dealt it;
                E ate it;
                    F fought for it;

G got it;
    H had it;
        I inspected it
            J joined it;
                K kept it;
                    L longed for it;
                        M mourned for it;

N nodded at it;
    O opened it;
        P peeped in it;
            Q quartered it;
                R ran for it;
                    S stole it;

T took it;
    V viewed it;
        W wanted it;
            X, Y, Z, and ampers-and,
                All wished for a piece in
                    hand.

Here we go up, up, up,
    And here we go down, down,
        downy,
Here we go backward and forward,
    And here we go round, round,
        roundy.

Tom, Tom, the piper's son,
Stole a pig, and away he run;
  The pig was eat,
    And Tom was beat,
And Tom ran crying down the street.

Jack and Jill went up the hill
    To fetch a pail of water;
Jack fell down and broke his crown,
    And Jill came tumbling after.

London Bridge is broken down,
Dance over my Lady Lee;
London Bridge is broken down,
With a gay lady.

How shall we build it up again?
Dance over my Lady Lee;
How shall we build it up again?
With a gay lady.

Build it up with silver and gold,
Dance over my Lady Lee;
Build it up with silver and gold,
With a gay lady.

Silver and gold will be stole away,
Dance over my Lady Lee;
Silver and gold will be stole away,
With a gay lady.

Build it up with iron and steel,
Dance over my Lady Lee;
Build it up with iron and steel,
With a gay lady.

Iron and steel will bend and bow,
Dance over my Lady Lee;
Iron and steel will bend and bow,
With a gay lady.

Build it up with wood and clay,
Dance over my Lady Lee;
Build it up with wood and clay,
With a gay lady.

Wood and clay will wash away,
Dance over my Lady Lee;
Wood and clay will wash away,
With a gay lady.

Build it up with stone so strong,
Dance over my Lady Lee;
Huzza! 'twill last for ages long,
With a gay lady.

As I was walking in a field of
        wheat,
I picked up something good to
        eat;
Neither fish, flesh, fowl, nor
        bone,
I kept it till it ran alone.

Wine and cakes for gentlemen,
        Hay and corn for horses,
A cup of ale for good old wives,
        And kisses for young lasses.

See, see! What shall I see?
A horse's head where his tail
        should be.

Little fishes in a brook,
Father caught them on a hook,
Mother fried them in a pan,
Johnnie eats them like a man.

Pussy cat, pussy cat, where have you been?
I've been to London to see the Queen.
Pussy cat, pussy cat, what did you there?
I frightened a little mouse under the chair.

Pat a cake, pat a cake, Baker's man;
So I do, master, as fast as I can.
Pat it and prick it and mark it with T,
And then it will serve for Tommy and me.

Little Boy Blue, come blow your horn,
The sheep's in the meadow, the cow's in the corn.
What! Is this the way you mind your sheep,
Under the haycock fast asleep?

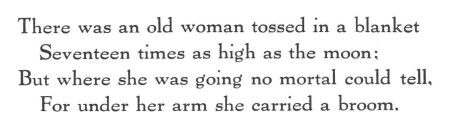

There was an old woman tossed in a blanket
    Seventeen times as high as the moon;
But where she was going no mortal could tell,
    For under her arm she carried a broom.

"Old woman, old woman, old woman," said I,
"Whither, ah whither, ah whither so high?"
"To sweep the cobwebs from the sky,
    And I'll be with you by and by."

My dear, do you know
How, a long time ago,
    Two poor little children,
Whose names I don't know,

Were stolen away
On a fine summer's day,
    And left in a wood,
As I've heard people say?

And when it was night,
So sad was their plight,
    The sun it went down,
And the moon gave no light!

They sobbed and they sighed,
And they bitterly cried,
    And the poor little things
They laid down and died.

And when they were dead,
The robins so red
    Brought strawberry leaves
And over them spread.

And all the day long
They sang them this song:
"Poor babes in the wood!
Poor babes in the wood!
    And don't you remember
The babes in the wood?"

A hill full, a hole full,
Yet you cannot catch a bowl full.

Rock-a-bye baby,
Thy cradle is green;
Father's a nobleman,
Mother's a queen,
And Betty's a lady
And wears a gold ring,
And Johnny's a drummer
And drums for the king.

If I'd as much money as I could
    spend,
I never would cry old chairs to
    mend,
Old chairs to mend, old chairs to
    mend;
I never would cry, old chairs to
    mend.
If I'd as much money as I could
    tell,
I never would cry old clothes to
    sell,
Old clothes to sell, old clothes to
    sell;
I never would cry, old clothes to
    sell.

Pussy-cat Mole jumped over a coal,
And in her best petticoat burnt a
    great hole.
Poor pussy's weeping, she'll have
    no more milk
Until her best petticoat's mended
    with silk.

Cold and raw the north winds blow
Bleak in the morning early,
All the hills are covered with snow,
And winter's now come fairly.

The man in the moon came down too soon
  To inquire the way to Norridge;
The man in the south, he burnt his mouth
  With eating cold plum porridge.

Four-and-twenty tailors
    Went to kill a snail;
The best man among them
    Durst not touch her tail;
She put out her horns
    Like a little Kyloe cow.
Run, tailors, run, or
    She'll kill you all just now.

Lucy Locket lost her pocket,
Kitty Fisher found it;
There was not a penny in it,
But a ribbon round it.

Old Sir Simon the king,
And young Sir Simon the squire,
And old Mrs. Hickabout
Kicked Mrs. Kickabout
Round about our coal fire.

❧

Round and round the rugged rock
The ragged rascal ran.
How many R's are there in that?
Now tell me if you can.

❧

Bessy Bell and Mary Gray,
They were two bonny lasses;
They built their house upon the lea,
And covered it with rushes.

Bessy kept the garden gate,
And Mary kept the pantry;
Bessy always had to wait,
While Mary lived in plenty.

❧

Swan, swan, over the sea;
Swim, swan, swim!
Swan, swan, back again;
Well swum, swan!

❧

There is a well
As round as an apple, as deep as a
    cup,
And all the king's horses can't fill
    it up.

As little Jenny Wren
Was sitting by her shed.
She waggled with her tail,
And nodded with her head.

She waggled with her tail,
And nodded with her head,
As little Jenny Wren
Was sitting by the shed.

❧

There was a little boy and a
    little girl
Lived in an alley;
Says the little boy to the little
    girl,
"Shall I, oh, shall I?"

Says the little girl to the little
    boy,
"What shall we do?"
Says the little boy to the little
    girl,
"I will kiss you."

❧

The boughs do shake and the bells
    do ring,
So merrily comes our harvest in,
Our harvest in, our harvest in,
So merrily comes our harvest in.

We've ploughed, we've sowed,
We've reaped, we've mowed,
We've got our harvest in.

Little Tom Tucker
Sings for his supper.
What shall he eat?
White bread and butter.
How will he cut it
Without e'er a knife?
How will he marry
Without e'er a wife?

"To bed, to bed," says Sleepy-Head;
"Let's stay awhile," says Slow;
"Put on the pot," says Greedy-Sot,
"We'll sup before we go."

Diddle, diddle, dumpling, my son John,
Went to bed with his breeches on,
One stocking off, and one stocking on,
Diddle, diddle, dumpling, my son John.

High diddle diddle,
The cat and the fiddle,
The cow jumped over the moon;
The little dog laughed
To see such craft,
And the dish ran away with the spoon.

If you sneeze on Monday, you
　　sneeze for danger;
Sneeze on a Tuesday, kiss a
　　stranger;
Sneeze on a Wednesday, sneeze for
　　a letter;
Sneeze on a Thursday, something
　　better.
Sneeze on a Friday, sneeze for
　　sorrow;
Sneeze on a Saturday, joy
　　tomorrow.

Margaret wrote a letter,
Sealed it with her finger,
Threw it in the dam
For the dusty miller.
Dusty was his coat,
Dusty was the silver,
Dusty was the kiss
I'd from the dusty miller
If I had my pockets
Full of gold and silver,
I would give it all
To my dusty miller.

Clap, clap handies,
　Mammie's wee, wee ain;
Clap, clap handies,
　Daddie's comin' hame;
Hame till his bonny wee bit laddie:
Clap, clap handies,
　My wee, wee ain.

Dance to your daddie,
　My bonnie laddie,
Dance to your daddie, my bonnie
　　lamb!
You shall get a fishie,
　On a little dishie,
You shall get a fishie when the
　　boat comes home.

Dance to your daddie,
　My bonnie laddie,
Dance to your daddie, and to your
　　mammie sing!
You shall get a coatie,
　And a pair of breekies,
You shall get a coatie when the
　　boat comes in.

Cocks crow in the morn
　To tell us to rise,
And he who lies late
　Will never be wise
For early to bed
　And early to rise
Is the way to be healthy,
　Wealthy and wise.

Oh where, oh where has my little
　　dog gone?
Oh where, oh where can he be?
With his ears cut short and his
　　tail cut long,
Oh where, oh where is he?

The two grey kits,
And the grey kits' mother,
All went over
The bridge together.

The bridge broke down,
They all fell in;
"May the rats go with you,"
Says Tom Bolin.

Robin and Richard
    Were two pretty men;
They stayed in bed
    Till the clock struck ten.
Then up starts Robin
    And looks at the sky:
"Oh, brother Richard,
    The sun's very high.
You go before
    With the bottle and bag,
And I will come after
    On little Jack nag."

Anna Maria she sat on the fire;
The fire was too hot, she sat on
the pot;
The pot was too round, she sat on
the ground;
The ground was too flat, she sat
on the cat;
The cat ran away with Maria on
her back.

Cobbler, cobbler mend my shoe
Get it done by half past two;
Stitch it up, and stitch it down,
Then I'll give you half a crown.

Thirty days hath September,
April, June, and November;
February has twenty-eight alone,
All the rest have thirty-one,
Excepting leap-year, that's the
time
When February's days are twenty-
nine.

The cock's on the housetop
blowing his horn;
The bull's in the barn a-threshing
of corn;
The maids in the meadows are
making of hay;
The ducks in the river are
swimming away.

Ladies and gentlemen come to
supper —
Hot boiled beans and very good
butter.

Christmas is coming, the geese are
getting fat,
Please to put a penny in an old
man's hat;
If you haven't got a penny a
ha'penny will do,
If you haven't got a ha'penny,
God bless you.

John Bull, John Bull,
Your belly's so full,
You can't jump over
A three-legged stool.

As I walked by myself,
And talked to myself,
Myself said unto me:
"Look to thyself,
Take care of thyself,
For nobody cares for thee."

I answered myself,
And said to myself
In the self-same repartee:
"Look to thyself,
Or not look to thyself,
The self-same thing will be."

Is John Smith within?—Yes, that he is.
Can he set a shoe?   Ay, marry, two.
Here a nail and there a nail,
Tick–tack–too.

I had a little hen, the prettiest ever seen,
She washed me the dishes and kept the house clean.
She went to the mill to fetch me some flour,
And always got home in less than an hour.
She baked me my bread, she brewed me my ale,
She sat by the fire and told many a fine tale.

When I was a little boy I lived by myself,
And all the bread and cheese I got I put upon a shelf;
The rats and the mice, they made such a strife,
I was forced to go to London to buy me a wife.
The streets were so broad and the lanes were so narrow,
I was forced to bring my wife home in a wheelbarrow;
The wheelbarrow broke and my wife had a fall,
And down came the wheelbarrow, wife and all.

'Twas once upon a time, when Jenny Wren was young,
So daintily she danced and so prettily she sung,
Robin Redbreast lost his heart, for he was a gallant bird,
So he doffed his hat to Jenny Wren, requesting to be heard.

"O, dearest Jenny Wren, if you will but be mine,
You shall feed on cherry pie and drink new currant wine,
I'll dress you like a goldfinch or any peacock gay,
So, dearest Jen, if you'll be mine let us appoint the day."

Jenny blushed behind her fan and thus declared her mind:
"Since, dearest Bob, I love you well, I take your offer kind;
Cherry pie is very nice and so is currant wine,
But I must wear my plain brown gown and never go too fine."

How many days has my baby to play?
Saturday, Sunday, Monday,
Tuesday, Wednesday, Thursday, Friday,
Saturday, Sunday, Monday.

Humpty Dumpty sat on a wall,
Humpty Dumpty had a great fall;
All the king's horses and all the king's men
Couldn't put Humpty Dumpty together again.

Three blind mice! See how they
    run!
They all ran after the farmer's
    wife,
Who cut off their tails with a
    carving knife.
Did you ever see such a thing in
    your life
As three blind mice?

❦

Sleep, baby, sleep,
Our cottage value is deep:
The little lamb is on the green,
With woolly fleece so soft and
    clean —
Sleep, baby, sleep.

Sleep, baby, sleep,
Down where the woodbines creep;
Be always like the lamb so mild,
A kind, and sweet, and gentle
    child.
Sleep, baby, sleep.

❦

One, he loves; two, he loves;
Three, he loves, they say;
Four, he loves with all his heart;
Five, he casts away.
Six, he loves; seven, she loves;
Eight, they both love.
Nine, he comes; ten, tarries;
Eleven, he courts; twelve, he
marries.

Here sits the Lord Mayor,
    Here sits his two men,
Here sits the cock,
    Here sits the hen,
Here sits the little chickens,
    Here they run in,
Chin chopper, chin chopper,
    Chin chopper, chin!

❦

As I was going to sell my eggs
I met a man with bandy legs,
Bandy legs and crooked toes;
I tripped up his heels,
And he fell on his nose.

❦

March winds and April showers
Bring forth May flowers.

❦

I see the moon,
    And the moon sees me;
God bless the moon,
    And God bless me.

❦

Nose, nose,
    Jolly red nose,
And what gave thee
    That jolly red nose?
Nutmeg and ginger,
    Cinnamon and cloves,
That's what gave me
    This jolly red nose.

Little King Boggen he built a fine hall,
Pie-crust and pastry-crust, that was the wall;
The windows were made of black puddings and white,
And slated with pancakes,—you ne'er saw the like!

As I went to Bonner
  I met a pig
    Without a wig,
Upon my word and honour.

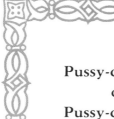

Pussy-cat ate the dumplings, the
     dumplings,
Pussy-cat ate the dumplings.
Mamma stood by, and cried, "Oh,
     fie!
Why did you eat the dumplings?"

There was a little woman, as I've
     been told,
Who was not very young, nor yet
     very old;
Now this little woman her living
     got
By selling codlins, hot, hot, hot!

Dickery, dickery, dare,
     The pig flew up in the air;
The man in brown soon brought
     him down,
     Dickery, dickery, dare.

You shall have an apple,
You shall have a plum,
You shall have a rattle,
When papa comes home.

Donkey, donkey, old and grey,
Open your mouth and gently bray;
Lift your ears and blow your horn,
To wake the world this sleepy
     morn.

Hannah Bantry,
In the pantry,
Gnawing at a mutton bone;
How she gnawed it,
How she clawed it,
When she found herself alone.

If you are to be a gentleman,
And I suppose you'll be,
You'll neither laugh nor smile,
For a tickling of the knee.

Ring-a-ring-a-roses,
A pocket full of posies;
Hush! hush! hush! hush!
We're all tumbled down.

One, Two—buckle my shoe;
Three, Four—open the door;
Five, Six—pick up sticks;
Seven, Eight—lay them straight;
Nine, Ten—a good fat hen;
Eleven, Twelve—I hope you're
     well;
Thirteen, Fourteen—draw the
     curtain;
Fifteen, Sixteen—the maid's in the
     kitchen;
Seventeen, Eighteen—she's in
     waiting;
Nineteen, Twenty—my stomach's
     empty.

Little Jack Horner
    Sat in a corner
Eating a Christmas pie;
    He put in his thumb,
    And pulled out a plum,
And said: "Oh, what a good boy am I!"

Miss Jane had a bag and a mouse was in it;
She opened the bag, he was out in a minute.
The cat saw him jump and run under the table,
And the dog said: "Catch him, Puss, soon as you're able."

The Queen of Hearts,
She made some tarts
All on a summer's day;
The Knave of Hearts,
He stole those tarts,
And took them clean away.

The King of Hearts
Called for the tarts,
And beat the Knave full sore;
The Knave of Hearts
Brought back the tarts,
And vowed he'd steal no more.

Goosey, goosey, gander, where dost thou wander?
Upstairs and downstairs and in my lady's chamber;
There I met an old man that wouldn't say his prayers,
I took him by his hind legs and threw him downstairs.

"I went up one pair of stairs."
"Just like me."

"I went up two pairs of stairs."
"Just like me."

"I went into a room."
"Just like me."

"I looked out of a window."
"Just like me."

"And there I saw a monkey."
"Just like me."

Mary had a pretty bird,
Feathers bright and yellow,
Slender legs – upon my word
He was a pretty fellow!

The sweetest note he always sung,
Which much delighted Mary.
She often, where the cage was
        hung,
Sat hearing her canary.

As I went through the garden gap,
Who should I meet but Dick
        Redcap!
A stick in his hand, a stone in
        his throat,
If you'll tell me this riddle,
I'll give you a groat.

St. Dunstan, as the story goes,
Once pulled the devil by his nose,
With red hot tongs, which made
        him roar,
That could be heard ten miles or
        more.

Terence McDiddler,
        The three-stringed fiddler,
Can charm, if you please,
        The fish from the seas.

A duck and a drake,
And a halfpenny cake,
With a penny to pay the old baker.
A hop and a scotch
Is another notch,
Slitherum, slatherum, take her.

Punch and Judy
Fought for a pie;
Punch gave Judy
A knock in the eye.
Says Punch to Judy,
Will you have any more?
Says Judy to Punch,
My eye is too sore.

Cry, baby, cry,
Put your finger in your eye,
And tell your mother it wasn't I.

See saw, Margery Daw,
    Jacky shall have a new master:
Jacky must have but a penny a day
Because he can work no faster.

Daffy-down-dilly is now come to town
With a petticoat green and a bright yellow gown.

"Cock, cock, cock, cock,
 I've laid an egg,
 Am I to gang ba-are-foot?"

"Hen, hen, hen, hen,
 I've been up and down
 To every shop in town,
 And cannot find a shoe
 To fit your foot,
 If I'd crow my hea-art out."

The lion and the unicorn
  Were fighting for the crown.
The lion beat the unicorn
  All about the town.
Some gave them white bread,
  And some gave them brown;
Some gave them plum-cake,
  And sent them out of town.

A frog he would a-wooing go,
    Heigh ho! says Rowley,
Whether his mother would let
    him or no.
With a rowley, powley,
    gammon and spinach,
    Heigh ho! says Anthony
    Rowley.

So off he set with his opera hat,
    Heigh ho! says Rowley,
And on the road he met with
    a rat.
With a rowley, powley,
    gammon and spinach,
    Heigh ho! says Anthony
    Rowley.

Pray, Mister Rat, will you go
    with me?
    Heigh ho! says Rowley,
Kind Mistress Mousey for to
    see?
    With a rowley, powley,
    gammon and spinach,
    Heigh ho! says Anthony
    Rowley.

They came to the door of
    Mousey's hall,
    Heigh ho! says Rowley,
They gave a loud knock, and
    they gave a loud call.
With a rowley, powley,
    gammon and spinach,
    Heigh ho! says Anthony
    Rowley.

Pray, Mistress Mouse, are you
    within?
    Heigh ho! says Rowley,
Oh yes, kind sirs, I'm sitting
    to spin.
    With a rowley, powley,
    gammon and spinach,
    Heigh ho! says Anthony
    Rowley.

Pray, Mistress Mouse, will you
    give us some beer?
    Heigh ho! says Rowley,
For Froggy and I are fond of
    good cheer.
    With a rowley, powley,
    gammon and spinach,
    Heigh ho! says Anthony
    Rowley.

As I was going to Derby
    Upon a market day,
I met the finest ram, sir,
    That ever was fed on hay.

This ram was fat behind, sir,
    This ram was fat before,
This ram was three yards high,
    sir,
    Indeed he was no more.

The wool upon his back, sir,
    Reached up unto the sky,
The eagles built their nests
    there,
    For I heard the young ones
    cry.

The wool upon his tail, sir,
    Was three yards and an ell,
Of it they made a rope, sir,
    To pull the parish bell.

The space between the horns,
    sir,
    Was as far as man could
    reach,
And there they built a pulpit,
    But no one in it preached.

This ram had four legs to walk
    upon,
    This ram had four legs to
    stand,
And every leg he had, sir,
    Stood on an acre of land.

Now the man that fed the ram,
    sir,
    He fed him twice a day,
And each time that he fed him,
    sir,
    He ate a rick of hay.

The man that killed the ram, sir,
    Was up to his knees in
    blood,
And the boy that held the pail,
    sir,
    Was carried away in the
    flood.

Indeed, sir, it's the truth, sir,
    For I never was taught to
    lie,
And if you go to Derby, sir,
    You may eat a bit of the
    pie.

Old King Cole
Was a merry old soul,
And a merry old soul was he;
He called for his pipe,
And he called for his bowl,
And he called for his fiddlers three.

Mistress Mary, quite contrary,
How does your garden grow?
With silver bells and cockle shells
And pretty maids all in a row.

I went to the toad that lies under
    the wall,
I charmed him out, and he came at
    my call;
I scratched out the eyes of the owl
    before,
I tore the bat's wing; what would
    you have more?

See a pin and pick it up,
All the day you'll have good luck.
See a pin and let it lay,
Bad luck you'll have all the day.

Hot-cross buns!
Hot-cross buns!
One a penny, two a penny,
Hot-cross buns!

If ye have no daughters,
Give them to your sons.
One a penny, two a penny,
Hot-cross buns!

Oh, I am so happy!
    A little girl said,
As she sprang like a lark
    From her low trundle bed.
It is morning, bright morning,
    Good morning, papa!
Oh, give me one kiss
    For good morning, mamma!

Diddlty, diddlty, dumpty,
The cat ran up the plum tree;
Give her a plum and down she'll
    come,
Diddlty, diddlty, dumpty.

As Tommy Snooks and Bessie
    Brooks
Were walking out one Sunday;
Says Tommy Snooks to Bessie
    Brooks,
"To-morrow—will be Monday."

Ride a cock horse to Shrewsbury
    Cross,
To buy little Johnny a galloping
    horse.
It trots behind and it ambles
    before
And Johnny shall ride till he can
    ride no more.

Now I lay me down to sleep,
I pray the Lord my soul to keep;
And if I die before I wake,
I pray the Lord my soul to take.

If wishes were horses,
    Beggars might ride;
If turnips were watches,
    I would wear one by my side.

Bonny lass, pretty lass,
  Wilt thou be mine?
Thou shalt not wash dishes
  Nor yet serve the swine.
Thou shalt sit on a cushion
  And sew a fine seam,
And thou shalt eat strawberries,
  Sugar and cream.

Handy-spandy, Jacky dandy,
Loves plum cake and sugar candy.
He bought some at a grocer's shop,
And pleased away went hop, hop, hop.

Ding—dong—bell, the cat's in the well.
Who put her in?   Little Johnny Green.
Who pulled her out?   Great Johnny Stout.
What a naughty boy was that
To drown poor pussy cat
Who never did him any harm,
And killed the mice in his father's barn.

This pig went to market,
That pig stayed at home;
This pig had roast meat,
That pig had none;
This pig went to the barn door,
And cried "week, week," for more.

Come when you're called,
Do what you're bid,
Shut the door after you,
Never be chid.

A was an archer,
    who shot at a frog;
B was a butcher,
    and had a great dog.
C was a captain,
    all covered with lace;
D was a drunkard,
    and had a red face.
E was an esquire,
    with pride on his brow;
F was a farmer,
    and followed the plough.
G was a gamester,
    who had but ill-luck;
H was a hunter,
    and hunted a buck.
I was an innkeeper,
    who loved to carouse;
J was a joiner,
    and built up a house.
K was King William,
    once governed this land;
L was a lady,
    who had a white hand.
M was a miser,
    and hoarded up gold;
N was a nobleman,
    gallant and bold.

O was an oyster girl,
    and went about town;
P was a parson,
    and wore a black gown.
Q was a queen,
    who wore a silk slip;
R was a robber,
    and wanted a whip.
S was a sailor,
    and spent all he got;
T was a tinker,
    and mended a pot.
U was a usurer,
    a miserable elf;
V was a vintner,
    who drank all himself.
W was a watchman,
    and guarded the door;
X was expensive,
    and so became poor.
Y was a youth,
    that did not love school;
Z was a zany,
    a poor harmless fool.

Blind man, blind man,
    Sure you can't see?
Turn round three times,
    And try to catch me.
Turn east, turn west,
  Catch as you can,
Did you think you'd caught me?
    Blind, blind man!

There were two blackbirds sitting on a hill,
One named Jack and the other named Jill.
Fly away, Jack!   Fly away, Jill!
Come again, Jack!   Come again, Jill!

Cross patch, draw the latch,
   Sit by the fire and spin;
Take a cup and drink it up,
   Then call your neighbours in.